ARROWS
of
FAITH

Sia Kuyembeh

www.trafford.com

North America & international
toll-free: 1 888 232 4444 (USA & Canada)
fax: 812 355 4082

CONTENTS

INTRODUCTION

When a person becomes a Christian and a new member of the Body of Christ (the family of God), by simply confessing with their mouth and believing in their heart that Jesus Christ of Nazareth is LORD, he or she now steps into a spiritual and physical battlefield of good versus evil. This battle between God and Satan is purely to possess and capture your very own soul. God the creator of all living flesh wills His creation (both men and women), to become believers in Him, and follow and worship Him all their days of their lives here on planet earth. God created all human beings to worship Him in Spirit and in Truth, and to accept His Only Son, Jesus Christ of Nazareth, the 'Messiah' as your personal LORD and Saviour. The enemy of God, Satan (Lucifer, Beelzebub), our adversary who roams around like a wounded lion seeking those whom he may devour, tries to possess us for his own purpose in capturing our soul because he knows how important our very soul is to our Creator—the LORD God Almighty. God never intended for anyone to go to hell where Satan's domain is—for hell was created for the devil, and all his fallen angels, and those who have not believed in Christ Jesus. Even, Jesus Christ of Nazareth during His three years of ministry here on earth spoke more about hell than he did about the kingdom of heaven to warn us all of the consequences of sin, and not believing in Him or His Gospel message of Salvation. The closer you are to God, the stronger the challenges you may be faced with. The day you choose to accept Jesus Christ as LORD, that same day you are being noted down and targeted in hell by Satan himself.

The question is: *Can you endure challenges for the sake of Jesus Christ, or will you give into the enemy's evil strategies to destroy Gods purpose for your life?*

Many times the choices we make during difficult everyday challenges can affect those we are directly or indirectly linked to on our destiny route. In the writing of this book, my aim and purpose is for you the reader is to get a fresh insight and fresh revelation Word from God, about why we all face challenging moments in life, and how God in His great grace and mercy restores us by the power of His great *'agape'* (unconditional) love. In the Old Testament **Book of Jeremiah, chapter 1 and verse 5,** of the Holy Bible (KJV) says: ***"Before I formed thee in the belly I knew thee; and before thou camest forth out of the womb I sanctified thee, and I ordained thee a prophet unto the nations".***

God knew us before we were even conceived, and has set each and everyone of us apart that is born on planet earth. Whatever challenges we are faced with in our everyday life it teaches us and gives us experience for what every man, woman, and child was born to accomplish, regardless of their age or ethic background or social status. However, many people never wait for God's divine and supernatural intervention in the mist of their trials; instead they are moved by their own inner emotions to deal with their circumstances according to the flesh. God has so many faithful promises in the Holy Bible to encourage us to be still and know that He is forever God, and can also do that which man thinks is impossible.

My own personal challenges started since the day I was conceived in my mother's womb. My earthly father and my earthly mother got separated. Many years later, he apologised.

Growing up without a biological parent can be a very difficult situation, especially not having a father-like-figure around to help you grow and mature in life but that is how I was unfortunately brought up in unpleasant circumstances. I am not here to tell you that my life has been a bed or roses of prosperity and success; I have had many a fair share of trials in my own life, and as a Christian I initially thought all Christians were exempt from trials and tribulation and tests of faith. I like so many Christians found out the hard way of how wrong I was to that untrue fallacy, for I know now through personal pain and suffering that Christianity has a cross to bear for every Christian believer.

I became a Christian at the age of 16, and during this year I was introduced to my real father. When we both met he could not stop forgiving himself and continuously kept apologising for all his selfish actions crying profusely. My mother who had a very difficult time, and no source of income coming in to our house from anywhere (now that her husband, my father had left us), allowed my grand-mother to look after me but she ended up giving me to an uncle as his own child to look after.

On the 10th of May 2003, I got married at the age of 25 to a man I truly and deeply loved, and we had three children (three sons). One of my sons Robin was diagnosed with a rare medical condition of Autism, in which he lost his speech at 2 years of age, and could hardly sense or understand anything concerning his natural surroundings. Robin's condition as my first born child broke my heart and almost made me suicidal, but in the mist of all these trials, tests of faith, sleepless nights of fear, worrying and many heart-searching questions I had asked God— God showed and proved to me (and is still doing so), that He was always with me, and my son Robin. My son is aged nine now, and by God's great grace, love and mercy is able to understand basic simple instructions now. After nine years of marriage, in December 2012, my husband and I got separated. Our marriage had unfortunately fallen apart, and because of my children the local authorities were now involved and told me firmly I had to leave my marital home on the 12th of the 12th, 2012. If I did not leave on this day, my children would have been taken away from me by the Social Services. So for the sake of my children I left my husband. I believe God was with me, and definitely had a hand in me making my final decision. God delivered me and gave me a brand new home for me and my children. During this period of my life, I attended a deliverance session at my local church where a guest preacher, an anointed man of God saw me crying and spoke these words to me: ***"Why are you crying, you should be thanking Him right now, for He has delivered you!"***

These were prophetic words of comfort and joy to my ears because God had used this Christian man to speak directly to my troubled and weary heart in a time of need. I was deeply relieved that someone had listened to my life story; my cries; my prayers; my tears; my discomfort; my fears and all my anxieties, and answered them in a unique miraculous way, praise God, AMEN!!!

A few months later after all this happened, I discovered my ex-husband got married again, and at the time of writing this my first book, I also found out that his new wife is pregnant. I do not hate my ex-husband neither do I regret having three children with him. Hate is another word described by God as likened to murder and the Holy Bible commands us all that we should not kill anyone. Time is the greatest healer. As for me and my children, we are in God's loving hands of care and protection, and in due process and progress we too shall all be fully delivered, healed and saved in Jesus Christ's name, AMEN!!!

I have forgiven my ex-husband wholeheartedly, and I sincerely pray and hope he truly finds the unconditional love and peace he and so many people long for in this world today, AMEN!!!

As for me I have learnt through my heartaches and pain and suffering that I am still a warrior of Christ in the army of the LORD; with a *never-say-die* attitude. A never-say-die attitude belongs to a warrior. A warrior never dies. A warrior presses for the mark of a higher calling. A warrior knows no defeat. A warrior gets up one more time. A warrior has a no stay in one place or put down attitude! King David of Israel was a mighty warrior, a man with a never-say-die attitude from an early age, because he had "faith-training" with a lion and a bear!

When you know who you are, when you know your life is hidden in Christ in God, there is no defeat! Failure is never final. King David only spoke 4 words, which you and I as warriors of Christ Jesus need to speak out in faith all the time over your enemies: *pursue, overtake and recover all!*

Despite the odds, despite people letting you down, despite people talking about you, despite people talking you out of your destiny, despite people speaking against your victory—you have to encourage yourself as David did. You have to have a never-say-die attitude. You have to be bold and say, "I will pursue, I will overtake and I will recover **all** that the devil has stolen from me, in Jesus Christ's mighty name!"

In Psalms 34 and 27, the Psalmist David wrote, however impossible it seems, however long it takes, I don't care—I will bless the LORD at all times! Remember the Old Testament story of King David and 600 of his men. Scriptures record they recovered all that the enemy had stolen from them. A true warrior belongs to the Lion of the Tribe of Judah, and he knows no defeat, because Jesus Christ of Nazareth is the Lion of the Tribe of Judah who is the Victorious One, who knows no defeat, because even death could not hold Him captive, even in the grave He **is** LORD!

A warrior with a never-say-die attitude has fire in his eyes, in his soul, in his body. A warrior boldly declares in the face of his enemies, I will live and not die, I will possess my land, I will maximise my potential. A warrior with a never-say-die attitude doesn't get lazy. He has a dream in his heart, and he knows you have to put faith into action. A warrior doesn't have a weak, spineless, no back-bone attitude. A warrior learns to stand on his own feet. A warrior fights his own battles. A warrior is trained and disciplined. A warrior is serious about his salvation. A warrior doesn't have a 'pity party' spirit!

Quit waiting on God and arise, wake up, get up, and get going because God's waiting on you. Don't be a cry-baby, or wait for someone to come and rescue you—be a warrior!

God's armies of never-say-die warriors are not lazy, weak or impassive; they are bold, persistent and endure to the very end of age! God is building a new army of warriors, who will always march to the beat of Jesus Christ, and possess their birthright, their destiny, their dream, their victory. These warriors are determined to possess their possessions; they are aggressive, their attitude is forever forward, and never going backwards!

ARE YOU A WARRIOR IN THE ARMY OF THE LORD?

All challenges (whether spiritual or physical) are won or lost in the mind. For this is the place of battle—the mind. This is where God and Satan to do battle with each other on a daily basis. Satan who is pure evil and the father of all lies tries to get his foothold—by invading your mind with wrong evil thought patterns, because Satan's very nature is to kill, steal, lie, cheat and destroy us while God who is holy and righteous invades our mind with pure thoughts of love, grace, mercy, compassion, forgiveness.

Whenever you are faced with a challenge it is essential to know how to deal with it. Your strength and weakness matter, but as Christians, God is our strength. Our weaknesses are made stronger as we rely on God for victory over life's challenges.

In this book, I have given examples of people who had difficult challenges. People like Job, who lost his children and riches, yet did not turn away from God. Instead, in the mist of all his trials he still trusted in God. Hannah who was barren and what many people believe to be past the ages of child-bearing trusted God for a child, and she never gave up her hope and faith in God for her miracle baby. And God blessed her with a son named Samuel who she dedicated back to God as a Prophet. Sarai (Sarah) the wife of Abraham, the father of all nations, waited for many years for a child, and eventually God blessed the fruit of her womb at the very ripe old age of 90!

How much more are you personally willing to wait on God to see you through as you encounter challenges in your life?

As Christians we are born to win. Jesus Christ of Nazareth won the battle for all mankind's sins, and gave us this victory 2,000 years ago when He carried His own broken, wounded, and bruised body to bear all our sins and to shed all of His precious blood on the Cross at Calvary Hill.

I hope by God's love and grace this book will restore your faith in God as you read it. And my prayer for you the reader is that God gives you total victory over every challenge that comes your way. Never give up or lose faith because the trying of our faith comes through trials and tests. God knows that we can be what He says and wills us to be.

God Bless you in Jesus' name, AMEN!!!

ACKNOWLEDGEMENTS

I want to thank the LORD God Almighty for His strength, His divine favour, His provision, and His great grace for making it possible for my dream to come true. It is by His awesome power and the leading of His Holy Spirit that the publishing of this book has been made possible. God is more than able to bring to pass all that we ask or think. Give me the grace my Father to serve you as long as I live, AMEN!

I would in all humility, sincerely like to thank my family and friends and everyone who helped or contributed in one way or another to put this book together. May God richly bless you and grant unto you all your hearts' desires, AMEN!

A special thank you goes to my blessed children who have loved me unconditionally, no matter what I put them through in other to achieve the publication of this book.

I also want to thank Evangelist Daniele Moskal who played a major role in providing his editorial and proof-reading skills to this book, and his wife Prophetess Moji for her moral support and their prayers. May the Almighty God grant you both immense supernatural favours as you help others to make their dreams possible, AMEN!

A special thank you to all my pastors and congregation members at *Living Glory Community Chapel,* for all their love, moral support, and prayers. May the LORD God Almighty richly reward you all in Jesus Christ's faithful name, AMEN!!!

Love in Christ,

Sia Kuyembeh

WHAT ARE TRIALS?

'Miriam-Webster' the online Encyclopedia Britannica's description and definition of the word **'Trial'** from a Christian viewpoint says it is*: "a test of faith, patience, or stamina through subjection to suffering or temptation; the action or process of trying or putting to the proof"*.

Trials come as unavoidable challenges in our daily lives helping us to understand full the gravity of certain decisions or actions taken by ourselves or others for a particular reason. For example: As a child I never grew up with my parents, I did not really know what it meant to have a mum or a dad; life was not very smooth for me. I went through a difficult childhood which I believe by God's grace shaped and molded me to who I am today. My childhood challenges were not caused by myself, but by the impact of my mother's decision affected me. My dad was never a father to me. I never saw him.

My Uncle and his wife raised me up. As I started to grow up and mature into a young woman, I decided to take my own opposite direction in searching for love and acceptance but instead God called me by His Spirit to His ways and spoke these words to me:

"My daughter, lay all your troubles upon my shoulder, and be still and know that I am your God!"

WHY DO PEOPLE GO THROUGH DIFFICULT CHALLENGES MORE THAN OTHERS?

It is clear that certain people go through difficult challenges in life than others, and they keep asking themselves over and over again: *"Is there a God?"* While others accept that there is a God, they often think He is partial. God has different plans and purposes for individuals, and each one of us goes through a process in order to be prepared for what lies ahead. Abraham one of the Old Testament patriarchs; a man of righteousness who was called a 'friend of God' trusted God through may trials of his faith, but his wife Sarai (SARAH) was barren for many years. This was a moment of trial for the Man of God. This was beyond his action.

Abraham's faith, was like Noah's 'a righteousness of faith', of which they became heirs. Abraham just like Noah walked a walk of faith. As to their lives, they lived by faith. As to their death, they died in faith. **The Book of GALATIANS 3:6** (very importantly says), Abraham was accounted righteous some four hundred and thirty years before the law was given to Moses, and, moreover, that this was by faith alone:

"Abraham believed God and it was accounted to him for righteousness". (Genesis15:6)

In the New Testament Abraham is seen as the exemplar, his believing as exemplary, and in him justification is set forth an example the radiance of which shines to the ends of the earth and to the closing days of time. More than any person and more than any other place—save, perhaps in the **Book of Habakkuk 2:4**, Abraham in **Genesis. 15:6** is cited to show the substance of the Gospel and the essence of the faith. It is true to say that to the Apostle Paul and the Gospel of Jesus Christ could not be properly be preached & taught, nor could faith in Jesus Christ be rightly be declared, without opening, enlarging, and applying the truth that *'Abraham believed God and it was converted to him for righteousness'*.

Here was Abraham, the Father of the faithful, the heir of the promises, the friend of God

Almighty, the one in whose hearing was sworn the oath of the Sovereign One, who heard his immutable counsel, saw the vision of the righteousness of faith, of Christ, of Christ crucified, of the resurrection from the dead of the heavenly country, and of the Holy City.

Here was the one in whom the Gospel was preached before to the heathen, the one in whom all nations should be blessed. Here was the father of all the children of promise, the one in whom the Gospel was ministered four hundred and thirty years before the law was given: in a word, here was the one of whom it was written, *'Abraham believed God, and it was counted to him for righteousness'*.

Abraham believed God, despite the darkness, despite the serpent, despite the fall, despite sin, despite the curse, despite death/murder, despite the judgement to come, he believed God. He believed God to overcome the darkness, the serpent, the fall, the sin, the curse, death, and the judgement to come which he feared. Like Noah, Abraham was moved with fear, knowing that God would judge the world in righteousness not by water for a generation but by fire for evermore, of which the fire fell upon Sodom and Gomorrah—Abraham having seen the country burning as a furnace with his own eyes—was but a token. Observing Noah's belief, Abraham looked for a spiritual ark by faith, an ark that would carry him and his seed through the coming deluge of eternal fire. Like Noah, Abraham built an altar, **Genesis 8:20; 12:7-8,** and **13:18**, becoming heir with him of the righteousness which is by faith **Hebrews 11:7**.

And how should Abraham know so much of Noah, that he should follow the faith of him who found grace in the eyes of the Lord, because for well over half a century, Abraham and Noah were contemporaries? By faith Abraham, when he was called to go out into a place which he should after receive for an inheritance, obeyed and went out knowing not where he went. By faith he sojourned in the land of promise, as in a strange country, dwelling in tents with Isaac and Jacob, the heirs with him of the same promise. Yes, by faith he went out into a place, the land of promise, but he never received it as an inheritance, he dwelt in it as in a strange country. What did he think of this, did his faith fail him? NO, for he looked through the earthly sign to the heavenly reality. He gazed beyond time into eternity. He saw past death to the resurrection and the new life. Hence Abraham endured as seeing Him who is invisible, receiving the promise of earthly Canaan as a heavenly pledge that he should be heir of the world to come **(ROMANS 4:13).**

In this world, Abraham received not so much as a foot's breadth of land. For all the promises, he had needs, a need to purchase a burying place, a graveyard, from the sons of Heth, to lie down to rest his wife. Abraham had nothing. No land. Despite the promise of God, he was after all a stranger in the land, a sojourner; he wandered as a nomad, dwelling in tents to the third generation. No land to build a house. No permanent building. No city for his posterity. Did this ancient patriarch Abraham still believe after all that? YES, by faith he *"looked for a city which hath foundations, whose builder and maker is God",* (HEBREWS 11:10).

Abraham's faith, the faith of God's elect was true and saving faith, the faith that comes from God alone, and could not fail. Nor shall any of his spiritual seed fail in Jesus Christ's faithful name, AMEN! Abraham, who rejoiced to see Christ's day, believed in the LORD when he met Melchizedek, **GENESIS14:18-20,** and gave him all tithes. What did Abraham see in this man Melchizedek (mystery man), that he should part with a tenth of all his income? And who was this that blessed even Abraham, for *'without all contradiction the less is blessed of the better'*? Indeed, who was this, said to be Abraham's better, and what did the friend of God, the father of the faithful see in him? Abraham saw one **'without father, without mother, without descent, having neither beginning of days, nor end of life; one made like unto the Son of God, abiding a priest continually'** (HEBREWS 7:3).

And Abraham believed in the Lord, and it was counted to him for righteousness. In the person of Melchizedek, by faith Abraham beheld the King in his beauty. The name Melchizedek is a compound which unites the Hebrew word for king, *'melek'*, with that for Righteousness, *'tsedeq'*. It is, by interpretation, King of righteousness. He reigned over human righteousness, legal righteousness, divine righteousness, (every form of righteousness): it was his royal gift. Righteousness, absolutely, was his dominion. It was his administration.

King of Salem, which is King of Peace, is what Melchizedek stood for. His was a dominion of peace. So righteousness and peace kissed each other. **<u>The basis of peace is righteousness established:</u>** Being justified by faith we have peace with God through our Lord Jesus Christ. This Prince of Peace, who reigned through righteousness upon Mount Zion, brought forth bread and wine, symbols of a broken body and shed blood to come, which should bring in everlasting righteousness. Melchizedek blessed Abraham saying, *'Peace be unto thee.'*

SARAH'S BARRENNESS

Genesis 18:11-12 King James Version (KJV)

[11] *"Now Abraham and Sarah were old and well stricken in age; and it ceased to be with Sarah after the manner of women.*

[12] *Therefore Sarah laughed within herself, saying, after I am waxed old shall I have pleasure, my LORD being old also?"*

(Sarai) Sarah which means "princess", the wife of Abraham laughed at the very thought of bearing children at such an advanced age—for Sarah had passed the age of childbearing, and was 90 years of age. But she may have laughed more out of pain than surprise when the three visitors (angels of God), visited Abraham. For in the ancient world, to be barren, as Sarah was, was considered grounds for divorce. Several women can be found in the Holy Bible illustrating the predicament of being a childless woman. Yet it's most interesting that each of those named below eventually did give birth to a child!

REBEKAH—in Genesis 25:21

Conceived after her husband Isaac prayed to the LORD on her behalf; she gave birth to twin boys, Esau and Jacob.

RACHEL—in Genesis 29:31-Genesis 30:24

Driven by despair, Rachel used her maid Bilhah to compete with the other wife of her husband Jacob, her older sister Leah; eventually Rachel gave birth to Joseph and later to Benjamin, whose birth caused her death.

MANOAH'S WIFE—in Judges 13

Told by God that she would conceive a son who would be a Nazarite; she gave birth to Samson, a judge of Israel.

HANNAH—1 Samuel 1

Desperately prayed for a son, whom she vowed to dedicate to the LORD; she gave birth to Samuel, a Prophet and judge of Israel.

ELIZABETH—Luke 1:5-25; Luke 57-66

Conceived after her husband Zacharias in a vision was promised a son who would be the forerunner to the Messiah; she gave birth to John the Baptist.

HANNAH THE
BARREN WIFE

Hannah was one of two wives of Elkanah, and they lived in the hill country of Ephraim. Elkanah's other wife had sons and daughters and year after year his other wife would provoke Hannah because the LORD did not give her any children. Hannah's husband did not understand why she was sad and <u>continuously wept</u> and would not eat. He believed that he was as valuable to her as ten sons. One day when Hannah could no longer bear the pain of her empty womb, she went to the temple to present her supplication to the LORD. She cried out to the LORD and wept bitterly. She was so upset that she made a promise to the LORD in her request for a son, she said:

 *"O Lord of hosts, if you will indeed look on the affliction of your servant and remember me and not forget*

your servant, but will give to your servant a son, then I will give him to the Lord all the days of his life, and no razor shall touch his head." (1 Samuel 1:1)

After she said this prayer out loud she continued to pray in her heart, but her lips moved. She was observed by the priest, Eli, who accused her of being a drunken woman. She explained that she had not had any wine nor strong drink and that instead she was deeply distressed and was praying to the LORD. Eli told her to go in peace and also asked that the LORD would grant her request. After that Hannah was no longer sad and she no longer fasted. Not long after her visit to the temple to present her request to the LORD, she was with child. When she delivered her son she called him Samuel which means "asked of God". Hannah did not forget her promise to the LORD either and as soon as Samuel was weaned she presented him to the LORD. When she arrived at the temple that same priest, Eli was there. Hannah reminded him of the time that she prayed to the LORD for a son and then dedicated Samuel to the LORD. And he worshiped the LORD there. Samuel was born as a gift and the result of the faithful <u>prayers</u> of his mother. His life through the first and second books of Samuel in the

Holy Bible is dominated by prayer. He goes on to become the last of the Judges. He constantly prayed for his people and this he learned from his dear mother, Hannah, a faithful woman of God.

IS GOD PARTIAL?

Is God partial? The answer is No! Yet many Christian people struggle to understand why they wholeheartedly serve God faithfully, but God still allows certain difficult things to happen to them. While others who don't really bother about God, seem to live a more comfortable life free from troubles. Well it is written in the Holy Bible in the (Book of Luke, chapter 12 and verse 48b) that: ***"For unto whomsoever much is given, of him shall be much required: and to whom men have committed much, of him they will ask the more!"***

For a Christian—the greater your own calling the more challenges you will unfortunately face in life. The LORD Jesus Christ never said we would not face afflictions or trials or tests of our faith or tribulation. God's Word clearly states this in the Book of Psalms, chapter 39, verse 11: ***"Many are the afflictions of the righteous: but the LORD delivereth him out of them all"***.

Dealing With
Difficult Challenges

In everyday life sooner or later you and I will find ourselves in a position somewhat like Job of the Old Testament. Job was considered to be a servant of God; there was no-one quite like Job upon the face of the earth who was blameless and upright, who feared God and shunned evil according to the Holy Scriptures of the Book of Job. Job was involved in a cosmic test between God and Satan, a contest that was proposed in heaven but staged on earth. In this extreme test of faith, Satan claimed that faithful, and in-right-standing with God people like Job the best man on earth who loved God, only love God because of the good things He provides. Satan put God and Job to the test by making Job suffer many of the worst calamities a person can endure. Satan suggested to God that if you remove the good things Job had received from Him, then Job's faith would eventually fade away together with all his riches and health. The

LORD God Almighty, the El-Shaddai God's reputation was now on the line. Would Job continue to trust his God, even while his life was going to suddenly fall apart? This is a most crucial question that Job and Christians who are faced with trials have to ask themselves: *"Will they leave God, or turn away from Him and follow someone else?"*

Even Job's wife mocked him, ***"Are you still holding on to your integrity? Curse God and die!"*** (Job 2:9)

Moreover, his friends were far crueler: they argued that Job was being punished, and that he fully deserved all of his tragedies crashing into his daily life. Job for his part, struggled to do what many seemed impossible, he continued despite all the hardships to believe in a loving, caring and merciful God even though all the evidence pointed against such a God. Like all grieving persons, Job went through emotional cycles. He whined, exploded, cajoled, and collapsed into self-pity. He agreed with his friends, then shifted positions and contradicted himself. And occasionally he came up with a powerful statement of brilliant hope. Mainly, Job asked for one thing: an appearance by the

One and Only Person who could explain his miserable fate—God Himself!

Job wanted to meet God face-to-face, and eventually Job got his deepest wish; God showed up in person. And when God finally spoke, no one—not even Job or any of his closest friends were prepared to what God had to say! I and probably you the reader of this book has had a similar trial or test of your faith like Job's at a time in your life. Your world seems to crumble and cave in on you. Nothing seems to make sense anymore, and on top of all this mess God seems distant and silent. At such moments of great crisis, trials and tests of faith, each one of us is put on trial. How could it happen, how did it happen? What did I do to deserve all this misery . . . . all this suffering . . . . all this abuse? Why me, LORD?

I'm sure Job who believed God, and never denied His power must have asked similar questions like the ones above. All most everyone, I repeat almost everyone on planet earth asks questions when terrible suffering occurs. Whether a car accident, a diagnosis of cancer or an incurable disease. The entire Book of Job deals with that philosophical question that one question, you know the one: **"WHY?"**

The Book of Job however ends on a remarkable note of surprises though. Job's friends, who had spouted all the right pieties and clichés, ask for forgiveness while Job himself who had raged and cried out, is given *'double'* blessings for all of his troubles—twice as much as he ever had before and died old and full of years!!!

When Apostle Paul wrote about suffering, he concentrated not merely on the pain itself, but on what qualities it produced in those who had faith. In **2 Corinthians, chapter 7 verse 11,** Paul cites the emotional suffering the Corinthians had experienced because of his letter addressed to them. All though the suffering was unpleasant, it undoubtedly produced something of great value: an abrupt change in their attitudes.

Apostle Paul had seen and experienced on many occasions the down side of life. He had been beaten several times, imprisoned on numerous occasions, ship-wrecked, but Paul despite all his personal trials and sufferings and tests of faith had discovered a secret for contentment in all situations: his deeply personal sense of living in and for Jesus Christ. In this he found the strength to handle anything life through at him, as Paul wrote: ***"I can do everything***

through Him (Christ) who gives me strength!"
(PHILIPPIANS 4:13 NIV)

Also, in the Book of Philippians chapter four, and verse four, Paul also writes: *"Rejoice in the LORD always!"*

When Paul said this, he was actually living and sleeping in a prison cell. His back flogged. His body starved, and a death sentence hanging over his head. He wasn't consulting his own surroundings, and neither was he consulting his own feelings. He looked beyond all of this and fixed his eyes on Jesus Christ of Nazareth, his *Sustainer* and his *Source*. Prison bars could not lock the Master out! What divine fellowship and faith Apostle Paul had in a God that met all his needs according to His glorious riches in Christ Jesus.

Today, do not despair; do not give up but look up and start rejoicing in the LORD God Almighty. For when the dust settles, He's all you have really got anyway! He's the Source; He's the Problem Solver—He's the Way Maker! So fix your eyes on Jesus Christ, the author, perfector, developer and finisher of your faith! Build something that will outlast bricks, mortar, popularity and public acclaim! Building a relationship with God is solid rock and will stand up to the storms of life because it is more stable than building on sinking sand. A wise person should always plan and charter their life ahead on God's principles and His Word.

In the Book of **2 Thessalonians, chapter 1, verse six,** Apostle Paul answers the question that most people have pondered or spoken about at some point of their lives: "IS LIFE UNFAIR?"

This question always bothers nearly everyone, young and old, rich and poor, black or white, educated or uneducated, who gets persecuted or who sees someone profit from wrong-doing. Apostle Paul in his day would have probably answered this question, *"Yes, but only temporarily!"*

Apostle Paul had the firm conviction deep down in his soul, that one day God would indeed turn the tables around on the unfairness of life—for God is the God of turn-around situations. He turns around everything from bad to good to the glory of His name on a daily basis. God is our *'Bridge over troubled waters'*; He is our *'Anchor in stormy seas'*; He is our *'Living Bread'* when we are hungry, our *'Living water'* when we are thirsty! When troubles calls on you, then call on God—for He is our *'Strong Tower'*; our *'Rock'*, our *'Fortress'*, our *'Deliverer'*, our *'Buckler'*, our *'Weapon'* in battle. For the battle is the LORD'S but the victory is ours! Faith is trusting and relying on God, no matter what the circumstances are! God does not guarantee anyone on planet earth a life of luxury and ease. Being a Christian and living as a Christian in today's modern society requires tough faith: a constant commitment to hang on and believe God against all the odds no matter what?

WHAT IS TRUE GENUINE FAITH?

Every effort of God has one focus—to find somebody who will believe Him. God wants you to approach Him with boldness and reverential fear when you have a need. He wants to be trusted! What parent doesn't? When you ask God something, you are acknowledging His awesome Sovereignty, His awesome wisdom and your total dependence on Him!

The **Book of Matthew, chapter seven and verse 7** says:

"Ask, and it shall be given you; seek, and ye shall find; knock, and it shall be opened unto you."

In the New Testament Book of Hebrews, the author concludes faith as resembling a difficult race. Like a runner, who has his or her eyes on the winner's prize, and, despite all nagging temptations to slacken the pace, absolutely refuses to let up until he or she crosses the finish line! What is true genuine faith and how can you be sure you've really got it? Some not all Christians think of faith as some kind of mysterious, magical force: if you muster up enough of it, you will quickly get rich, stay healthy and live a happy contented life.

"And we know that all things work together for good to them that love God, to them who are the called according to his purpose". Romans chapter eight, verse eight is a Scripture verse we can easily quote to someone else. What about when it's *your* turn to suffer? Is there really comfort found in this verse when it seems all hell is breaking loose in your daily life? Notice two important things you have to consider what Apostle Paul versed in the above Scripture:

1) All things work together for good but not all things are good. The loss of a job, a boss who is tyrannical, physical illness, or family troubles are not good things per se. In fact, often they are the direct result of evil. That's something important to observe. God never promised His beloved believers they would be immune from the problems and pains of this world.

Every day, unfortunately we must put up with much that isn't good. Turn on the television to watch the news—and most of it is bad news!

2) Nevertheless, good can come out of bad! **Romans 8:28** also promises that God uses all the circumstances of our lives—both the good, the bad and the downright ugly—to shape outcomes that will accomplish His purposes for us. And God's purposes and plans can only be good, because He is good by definition. **(JAMES 1:17)**

By affirming your trust and faith in God's power and presence; aligning your goals and visions with God's purposes and accepting the reliability of God's promises (which are 'Yes' and 'Amen'), can the verse of **Romans chapter eight, and verse eight** work for you in facing tough, every day troubled times!

Some people say it doesn't really matter what you believe, as long as you do the right thing. However, God's Word contradicts that sort of thinking. God knows that people become what they think, and that everything they do in life is shaped by what they believe! That's why believers need to pay particular careful attention to the teaching they receive.

Does it square up with Holy Scriptures?

Does it honour Jesus Christ?

Does it acknowledge what Apostle Paul wrote in the **Book of Titus, chapter 1 and verse 1?**

"The truth which accords with godliness"

We unfortunately live in a society of the *"fast track"*, the *"sound bite"*, "the *"hurried child"*, and the *"microwave quick mentality spirit.* But what is so attractive about the rush to achieve quick results? Is this how life was intended to be? By studying and meditating on God's Word, God shows us that He wants us to be <u>someone</u> rather than to get <u>somewhere</u>!

Rather than measuring our worth through personal achievements and acquisitions, God evaluates our true character, looking for such virtues as peace, truth, serenity, and strength of character. He values us for who we are and who we are becoming. He wants us to be using the New Testament Book of James:

1) People who can endure tests and trials.
2) People who trust God to provide for their needs and feel free to ask for His help.
3) People who can discern between good and bad choices and make wise decisions.
4) People who give and lend generously to others, just has God has given generously to us.
5) People who listen well and respond thoughtfully.
6) People who act instead of just talking and whose actions benefit others.
7) People who value and show compassion toward others who are in need, especially those forgotten by society.

It takes time to develop character like that. But God is interested in long-term growth, not just a quick fix! We may need to slow down and take a long, hard look at the direction of our lives. If we are driven to gain as much as we can as fast as we can, then we are heading down a pothole road toward devastating destruction! Times of great loss of suffering can provide a valuable opportunity for reflection and self-examination. For example, the loss of a loved one, a bad abusive marriage often brings back vivid memories that give insight into the meaning of the person's life. The same principle applies to

Christians today. In our darkest moments, in times of great loss or fear, God would have us pursue insight and self-examination.

Only faith changes people. For faith makes people see everything in a fresh new light. Their ears open to hear, their eyes open to see, and their hearts start to feel something completely different to what everyone else perceives. Faith is living and powerful. It's not a simple-minded thought or idea. It does not float around in a person's heart like a child's rubber-duck on water. Rather, it's like water that's been heated in a kettle. After switching on the kettle and the water is heating up, the water becomes different; its still water but it's now boiling hot. The same thing happens when God's Holy Spirit comes into our lives at the new birth of being *'born again'* into Jesus Christ (**JOHN 3:3 KJV**). It gives us faith that transforms our minds and attitudes, and creates within us an entirely new person.

[3] *"Jesus answered and said unto him, Verily, verily, I say unto thee, Except a man be born again, he cannot see the kingdom of God".*

Faith is active, profound and powerful. If I were to correctly describe faith to you now, I would say it's a daily process, not a result. In other words, faith changes the heart and mind of a person. Our intellectual reason tends to concentrate on what is present—the *'here and now'*, but faith concerns itself with things that are tangible and, contrary to intellectual reasoning, regards them as actually being present. This is why faith isn't as common among people as the *'five senses'* we have are. Considering the number of people there are alive in the world today (over 7 billion people), there are relatively few believers. Most people unfortunately concern themselves more with what they can see now, touch now, and handle right now, rather than listening or obeying God who gave man life and His Living Word, who is Christ Jesus.

Psalm 23:4 King James Version (KJV)

 [4] *"Yea, though I walk through the valley of the shadow of death, I will fear no evil: for thou art with me; thy rod and thy staff they comfort me"*.

Even though King David the sweet Psalmist of Israel couldn't see or hear the LORD, David said in the above Psalm: *"You are with me".* The LORD'S presence cannot be perceived by the five senses. Only faith enables a person to know that God is with us. Faith convinces a person that the LORD is nearer to us than we are to ourselves. You may be asking yourself right now, *'In what way is God near to me?'*

He is near to us through His Word! When King David wrote Psalm 23, he wrote: *"Your rod and Your staff give me courage"*; it's as if David wanted to say: *"Nothing else on planet earth can help me get through all my worries and troubles. God's Word alone is my rod and staff of protection. I will hang onto it and use it to pull myself back up again. I am certain that the LORD is with me, and that He gives me courage in all my anxieties and troubles. He defies the devil and the world, and He rescues and protects me from all my enemies!"*

David was referring to the image of a good shepherd tending his sheep, when he spoke these words, *"Your rod and Your staff".* He wanted to describe to us that God is the *'Good Shepherd'*, the *'Chief Shepherd,* and the *'Great Shepherd'* that guides His sheep with

His rod and staff—leading them to graze in the lush green meadows and drink fresh water. God also uses His staff to protect His sheep from all evil dangers. This is the way of the LORD—the True Shepherd who leads and guides us (the sheep of His pasture), with His staff. In other words, God leads us with His Word, which protects us from all spiritual and physical dangers and rescues us from all our enemies, and the fiery darts of Satan. Knowing this that God and His infallible, everlasting, Word so will richly strengthen and comfort us that no spiritual or physical trial seems too much to endure and overcome when we put our firm faith and clear conscience in Him is a wonderful thing to know.

Faith makes God real to us and real in us. Without faith, God's honour, glory, wisdom, righteousness, truth, grace, compassion, mercy, and forgiveness cannot be in us. Where there is no faith, God has no majesty, sovereignty or divinity. God does not require anything more from us than to just simply acknowledge His divinity and give Him all the due necessary reverence, glory, honour and praise He so richly deserves. We should never think of God as an idol but as Almighty God—the Almighty God Who accepts us and hears us when we cry out to Him; who is merciful to us, and Who stands by us through all our trials and tests of faith. When we honour God, His Sovereignty remains complete and intact. When we honour God in this way, we are showing the greatest wisdom, the highest justice, and the best worship and praise while offering the most pleasing pot-pourri, sweet-smelling sacrifices, AMEN!!!

MURPHY'S LAW

'Murphy's Law', this old adage states that:
"If something can go wrong, it will!"

Usually, we don't have to go looking for trouble; it seems to somehow find us on its own. Not that the struggles most of us face are anything like that of Job of the Old Testament confronted. But unfortunately we still have plenty of reminders that life is less than perfect: Illnesses, heartaches, divorces, and break-downs in our relationships, disappointments in our careers, the death of friends and loved ones, natural disasters, wars, famine. If we live long enough and remain honest and sincere then sooner or later we are compelled to reach the same conclusion that Job, and all his companions came to as they sat around Job's ash heap: ***"Man is born to trouble as the sparks fly upwards!"***

Some people will go to great lengths to avoid pain. Job encourages us to accept the troubles of everyday life, facing them squarely on, and turning to God in the midst of them. And if by God's great grace we would be fortunate enough to bypass some of the worst evils in this world then the most appropriate response is a heart of thankfulness, as well as love and compassion for those with a more common experience.

God saw you when you where in your mother's womb.

Psalm 139:13-16
New International Version (NIV)

[13] *"For you created my inmost being; you knit me together in my mother's womb.*

[14] *I praise you because I am fearfully and wonderfully made; your works are wonderful, I know that full well.*

[15] *My frame was not hidden from you when I was made in the secret place, when I was woven together in the depths of the earth.*

[16] *Your eyes saw my unformed body; all the days ordained for me were written in your book before one of them came to be.*

He knew your mother and father, and the circumstances of the home where you were to grow up. He knew the infant, junior, high school, college or university you would attend, and the neighbourhood in which you would live. God gave you and every person on planet earth the ability to survive, and walked with you through troubled times, good times and bad. He gave you survival techniques and ministering guardian angels to keep and protect you.

Psalm 139:11—King James Version (KJV)

[11] ***"For he shall give his angels charge over thee, to keep thee in all thy ways"***. He chose you before the foundation of the world to be holy and without blame before Him in love.

Ephesians 1:4 King James Version (KJV)

[4] *"According as he hath chosen us in him before the foundation of the world,*

that we should be holy and without blame before him in love".

He cried with you when you cried. He laughed with you when you laughed. He was grieved when you were misunderstood and treated unfairly. He watched and waited patiently, looking forward to the day when you would receive Jesus Christ of Nazareth as your LORD and Saviour.

John 1:12 Amplified Bible (AMP)

[12] *"But to as many as did receive and welcome Him, He gave the authority (power, privilege, right) to become the children of God, that is, to those who believe in (adhere to, trust in, and rely on) His name".*

God longs for your sweet fellowship, desiring for you to know Him more and more intimately. Your survival techniques were probably a lot different than mine. Whatever they were, and whatever your life may have been like up to this point, the peace of God can change the regrets and the wounds of the past into thanksgiving and praise. Just trust Him for He is the Only

One who can turn around everything from bad in your life for good, to the glory of His holy and anointed name!

Galatians 4:6 King James Version (KJV)

 [6] *"And because ye are sons, God hath sent forth the Spirit of his Son into your hearts, crying, Abba, Father".*

When in the middle of a trial or a conflict—from my own experiences as a Christian it can be quite difficult to call out to God and it can also take a lot of effort to hold on to God's Word. During these times, some of us cannot perceive God. We don't see Him, and our heart does not seem to feel His tangible presence or His help during an attack. Some even may think to themselves that God has left them during all these trials, so they now feel the power of sin and the weakness of their bodies, and some even start to doubt God's very existence. Many of us too have experienced the flaming arrows of the enemy (the devil, Satan), and the terrors of death. However, in the midst of all what seems to be taking place in our lives; our Helper; our Teacher, our Guide, our Comforter, and our

Advocate—the HOLY SPIRIT within our hearts begins to call out in you—*"ABBA, Father"*.

When in a prison jail, Joseph of the Old Testament struggled with becoming impatient and kept complaining after he was forgotten by the chief cupbearer to the Pharaoh of Egypt, who Joseph had interpreted a dream. When the devil saw all this, he attacked Joseph's mind with even more fiery darts and arrows. Jesus Christ Himself also felt these same arrows when the devil tempted Him in the wilderness after 40 days and 40 nights, saying: *"If thou be the Son of God, command that these stones be made bread"*. (Matthew 4:3)

Believers in Christ can always remain confident even in the worst possible dangers and hardships because God is a covenant keeping-seeking God, Who has promised to take care of us.

1 Peter 5:7 King James Version (KJV)

[7] *"Casting all your care upon him; for he careth for you"*.

It's important for Christians to be tested by trials, for without these tests their faith would wax cold and grow weak. A person's faith could eventually disappear completely. But if it is tested with hardships, Christians will truly discover what genuine faith is, and will be strengthened in their knowledge of Christianity. They will by God's great grace become stronger that even when troubles or anxieties occur, they will count it all joy, whether in good times or in bad times—looking at each hardship as if it were a cloud or fog that will soon vanish.

DEUTERONOMY
CHAPTER 6

¹ "Now these are the commandments, the statutes, and the judgments, which the LORD your God commanded to teach you, that ye might do them in the land whither ye go to possess it:

² That thou mightest fear the LORD thy God, to keep all his statutes and his commandments, which I command thee, thou, and thy son, and thy son's son, all the days of thy life; and that thy days may be prolonged.

³ Hear therefore, O Israel, and observe to do it; that it may be well with thee, and that ye may increase mightily, as the LORD God of thy fathers hath promised thee, in the land that floweth with milk and honey.

⁴ Hear, O Israel: The LORD our God is one LORD:

5 And thou shalt love the LORD thy God with all thine heart, and with all thy soul, and with all thy might.

6 And these words, which I command thee this day, shall be in thine heart:

7 And thou shalt teach them diligently unto thy children, and shalt talk of them when thou sittest in thine house, and when thou walkest by the way, and when thou liest down, and when thou risest up.

8 And thou shalt bind them for a sign upon thine hand, and they shall be as frontlets between thine eyes.

9 And thou shalt write them upon the posts of thy house, and on thy gates.

10 And it shall be, when the LORD thy God shall have brought thee into the land which he sware unto thy fathers, to Abraham, to Isaac, and to Jacob, to give thee great and goodly cities, which thou buildedst not,

11 And houses full of all good things, which thou filledst not, and wells digged, which thou diggedst not, vineyards and olive trees, which thou plantedst not; when thou shalt have eaten and be full;

[12] *Then beware lest thou forget the* LORD, *which brought thee forth out of the land of Egypt, from the house of bondage.*

[13] *Thou shalt fear the* LORD *thy God, and serve him, and shalt swear by his name.*

[14] *Ye shall not go after other gods, of the gods of the people which are round about you;*

[15] *(For the* LORD *thy God is a jealous God among you) lest the anger of the* LORD *thy God be kindled against thee, and destroy thee from off the face of the earth.*

[16] *Ye shall not tempt the* LORD *your God, as ye tempted him in Massah.*

[17] *Ye shall diligently keep the commandments of the* LORD *your God, and his testimonies, and his statutes, which he hath commanded thee.*

[18] *And thou shalt do that which is right and good in the sight of the* LORD: *that it may be well with thee, and that thou mayest go in*

and possess the good land which the LORD *sware unto thy fathers.*

19 To cast out all thine enemies from before thee, as the LORD *hath spoken.*

20 And when thy son asketh thee in time to come, saying, What mean the testimonies, and the statutes, and the judgments, which the LORD *our God hath commanded you?*

21 Then thou shalt say unto thy son, We were Pharaoh's bondmen in Egypt; and the LORD *brought us out of Egypt with a mighty hand:*

22 And the LORD *shewed signs and wonders, great and sore, upon Egypt, upon Pharaoh, and upon all his household, before our eyes:*

23 And he brought us out from thence, that he might bring us in, to give us the land which he sware unto our fathers.

24 And the LORD *commanded us to do all these statutes, to fear the* LORD *our God, for our good always, that he might preserve us alive, as it is at this day.*

²⁵ And it shall be our righteousness, if we observe to do all these commandments before the LORD our God, as he hath commanded us.

When you read the above chapter of Scripture verses it teaches us to put our trust in a God that will take care of us in both good and bad times. We should not become over confident in times of plenty, but we also need to be patient— enduring times of adversity for God will never leave us or forsake us. He will be near us in our troubles. Unbelievers don't have this confidence in God because the majority of them put their trust in earthly materialistic things. If what we need isn't available to us, we have to rely on God's faithful promises. If we do not rely on God, we are putting Him to the test. At Massah, Israel complained and asked: *"Is the LORD with us or not?"*

Here, the people did not trust God's promises because He didn't fulfill them in their own time, place or manner that they were expecting. Therefore, they gave up and stopped believing. When we try to dictate to God a particular time, a particular place, and a particular manner for Him to act, we are simply testing Him. Doing all this puts limits on God, and tries to force or make Him to do what we want. This is nothing less than to deprive God of His divine Sovereignty. But we must realize that God is free, and definitely not subject to any limitations. He is God, and He must be the One to let us know under His terms, the place, the manner, and the time He intervenes. In difficult times, we may not be able to believe God strongly or praise Him whole heartedly, and pray to Him as sincerely as we do in good times of prosperity and good health. However, we should at least believe and pray as much as we are able to.

Luke 18:1 King James Version (KJV)

 18 *"And he spake a parable unto them to this end, that men ought always to pray, and not to faint"*.

OUR SOURCE OF VICTORY

John 16:33 King James Version (KJV)

³³ *"These things I have spoken unto you, that in me ye might have peace. In the world ye shall have tribulation: but be of good cheer; I have overcome the world".*

Everyone should learn to remind themselves of Jesus Christ's victory. In Christ, we already have everything we need in life. If you the reader of this book confess to be a Christian, then you should only be living to spread and fulfill the Gospel message of victory to others as Christ commissioned us to do so, to very person whom you come into contact with on a daily basis. With the Word in us as an example, we should seize the opportunity to tell them about the victory that Jesus Christ secured for us and gave us. Christ the Victorious One accomplished everything on the Cross at Calvary Hill. No-one needs to add anything to it or subtract anything from it. We cannot or we do not need to wash away our own sins, or try to conquer death or the devil. Everything was completed for us by Jesus Christ of Nazareth; for He disarmed, destroyed and defeated the evil ruler of this world (Satan) 2,000 years ago at the Cross when Christ shed His precious blood for all mankind's sins—praise God, AMEN! May God continue to help us also to hold onto Christ's victory during our troubles and when we are dying? For in Christ Jesus we have a 'VICTOR' who gave us victory over the world, death, and the devil!!!

Revelation 12:11 King James Version (KJV)

 *"And they overcame him by the blood of the Lamb and by the word of their testimony; and they loved not their lives unto the death".*

The Holy Bible speaks of suffering as being engulfed by fire or tested by fire. Peter a Disciple of Jesus Christ said that we should not become upset or think it strange when we experience this fire. We are tested by fire, just as gold is refined in the furnace by fire. When we begin to believe in God, He does not abandon us but He lays a holy cross upon our backs and gives us His Holy Spirit within us to strengthen our faith. The Gospel is an awesome, powerful Word—the Word of God, but it cannot do its work in us without trials. No one can discover its power unless they experience it. The Gospel can only show its power where there is suffering. Because it is the Word of Life, it must therefore exercise all its power in death! If dying and death are absent, then it can do nothing, and no person would discover that it's stronger than sin and death!

Peter wrote in his first Epistle: *"Fiery troubles are coming in order to test you."* (1 Peter 4:12)

This fire or heat is the Cross and the suffering which makes you burn. For God inflicts this heavenly fire for no other reason except to test you, and your faith to see whether-or-not you are depending solely on Him, and upon His infallible, enduring Word. This is why God imposes the Cross on all His beloved believers, for He wants them to experience and demonstrate His awesome power. If you think believers (Christians) will only have good days on planet earth, while all unbelievers do not get to have any—well, unfortunately it does not work this way. Everyone, I repeat everyone experiences suffering.

Genesis 3:19 King James Version (KJV)

19 *"In the sweat of thy face shalt thou eat bread, till thou return unto the ground; for out of it wast thou taken: for dust thou art, and unto dust shalt thou return".*

God spoke the above words to Adam. And to Eve, God said this in:

Genesis 3:16 King James Version (KJV)

16 *"Unto the woman he said, I will greatly multiply thy sorrow and thy conception; in sorrow thou shalt bring forth children; and thy desire shall be to thy husband, and he shall rule over thee".*

Ever since the beginning of time; in the days of Creation of the first humans (Adam and Eve)— everyone that has ever lived shares in this same tragic condition of *'sin'*. Sin came into the world due to the unfortunate fall and disobedience of the first man and first woman in the Garden of Eden when they sinned against God by eating the forbidden fruit from the tree of life that God had warned Adam and Eve not to. Through the first man's sin, this made it all the more necessary for people like you and me reading this book to seek to repent and return back to God, and gain eternal life by accepting Jesus Christ (the last Adam), the 'Messiah', 'The Holy One of Israel', 'The Good Shepherd', 'The Great Redeemer', 'The Lion of the Tribe of Judah' and the Only One who can save us all—for salvation is found in no other name but the name of the LORD!!!

Acts 4:12 King James Version (KJV)

[12] *"Neither is there salvation in any other: for there is none other name under heaven given among men, whereby we must be saved"*.

Reading the remarkable story of Noah and the saving of entire family gives us a model of faith, patience and perseverance. It teaches us to put our sole trust and belief in God for total victory, and it also makes us aware of our need for patience.

But patience is unnecessary if we have no personal struggles or doubts. Even Jesus Christ of Nazareth warns us all to persevere in difficult situations with these words found in the New Testament in the **Book of Matthew 24:13 (KJV)**.

 [13] *"But he that shall endure unto the end, the same shall be saved"*.

Being trapped and enclosed inside a very large floating wooden container ship was no joke, and could hardly be described as having fun with all the sweat and stink of all the world's animals. Noah and his family saw and witnessed the huge deluge of water cataracts and downpours of torrential rain that tossed their ark of refuge and shelter to and fro; backwards and forwards on ever-rising floodwaters for days. Noah and his family were able to overcome their feelings of abandonment only through faith and belief that God was with them to conquer all their fears and anxieties. Yes, it came with tremendous struggles in their human nature but God showed Noah and his family love and compassion. In the same way a Christian who wants to live a pure, holy and virtuous life must desire within them to make a determined effort to control their sinful desires and rely on God to give them total victory. Unfortunately, we are not 'superhuman'—our human nature is weak and prone to sin. It cannot tolerate the very idea that God may have forgotten or abandoned us. We are even quick in wanting to brag and boast, and take all the credit and applause for ourselves when God does remember us by looking on us with loving kindness, giving us prosperity and good health. It's no wonder that we become hopeless and feels like God has abandoned us and everything seems to be going wrong?

No one living on planet earth should run away from Jesus Christ or from God the Father of all flesh. For God wills and wants us all to repent and return back to Him; sticking and staying close to Him 24/7—in the same manner in which small chicks gather under the comforting fluffy wings of a mother hen. Just as children cling to their beloved parents like Teflon, we should also find safety and refuge in Jesus Christ and our Heavenly Father, AMEN!

John 3:17 King James Version (KJV)

17 *"For God sent not his Son into the world to condemn the world; but that the world through Him might be saved"*.

This beautiful passage of Holy Scripture is something that you and I, and, everyone throughout the four corners of this earth should take these very words to heart because the LORD Jesus Christ is not a wicked judge. He is our *'Mediator'*, our *'Helper'*, our *'Comforter'*, and a *'Throne of Mercy and Grace'*. God is our *'Bishop of our Souls'*, our *'Brother in Arms'*, and our *'Intercessor'*. He is both our *'Heavenly Gift'*, and our *'Ever-Present Helper'*, in times of troubles and needs. But some of us have broken wounded hearts and minds from past trials, and sufferings that have not been healed and we, by our very own nature tend to distrust God. Yet, all of us should reflect, meditate, and study this above portion of Holy Scripture again and again, as a young child would—to learn that Jesus Christ did not come to judge the world but to save the world!

RENEWING YOUR MIND

The Book of First Beginnings, the Book of Genesis has a record that is most sobering to any reader who has probably asked themselves these questions at a stage in their own individual life: *"In light of all the Old Testament families represented, is there any hope for me in this present age? Is it worth even trying to build a happy, healthy, God-fearing and God-honouring home in today's evil society?"*

YES! I say a bold **YES again!** Because the problems of the families found in the Book of Genesis are only parts of the story. Family chaos and pain were neither God's original design nor was it the final word. With God's help and guidance, it is possible to create a comfortable and contented family home life that approaches God's intentions and His perfect will. That's why Holy Scriptures frequently encourage the LORD'S people to work towards making each family a community built on faith, love, hope, caring, restoration, blessings, grace, gentleness, patience, compassion, forgiveness, long-suffering, joy, peace, mercy, goodness and self-control which I truly believe are God's *'ARROWS OF FAITH'*.

Knowing who your enemy is

No matter whom we are or what we do for a living, all of us are bound to face struggles and conflicts in life. It could be any on of these: Financial pressures, bankruptcy, job losses, abuse, unemployment, marital problems, and abuse, divorce or separation, death, mortgage or rent arrears, addictions (alcohol, sex, pornography, drugs and gambling). When faced with setbacks like these above, most often people tend to blame God for all their circumstances, or other people, or even themselves. However, most people especially unbelievers are not aware that the Holy Bible urges every man and woman to consider another reason for all our struggles in life, that is a more evil sinister source, what Apostle Paul called the *"principalities"* and *"wicked powers"* in heavenly places. Our struggle our fight is not against God or other people (flesh and blood), but against *"spiritual hosts of wickedness",* against Satan (Lucifer, Beelzebub) our enemy and adversary—who is called the father of all lies; the evil serpent and the author of evil who hates God and Christianity, who accuses the brethren (believers of the Body of Christ) day and night who never has a rest day in attacking Christians.

Ephesians 6:11-12 King James Version (KJV)

[11] *"Put on the whole armour of God that ye may be able to stand against the wiles of the devil.*

[12] *For we wrestle not against flesh and blood, but against principalities, against powers, against the rulers of the darkness of this world, against spiritual wickedness in high places.*

Apostle Paul is clearing telling and warning us all that ultimately God and people are not our enemies, but sin and Satan are! If we intend to stand up to devil's continuous onslaughts and his adversaries, we must fight them on their own turf with the spiritual weapons that Almighty God has provided for every believer in Christ Jesus. These weapons are contained in the Full Armour of God in the **Book of Ephesians, chapter 6, verses 12-18.**

> Wherefore take unto you the whole armour of God, that ye may be able to withstand in the evil day, and having done all, to stand.
>
> Stand therefore, having your loins girt about with truth, and having on the breastplate of righteousness.
>
> And your feet shod with the preparation of the gospel of peace;
>
> Above all, taking the shield of faith, wherewith ye shall be able to quench all the fiery darts of the wicked.
>
> And take the helmet of salvation, and the sword of the Spirit, which is the word of God:
>
> Praying always with all prayer and supplication in the Spirit, and watching thereunto with all perseverance and supplication for all saints.
>
> For we wrestle not against flesh and blood, but against principalities, against powers, against the rulers of the darkness of this world, against spiritual wickedness in high places.
>
> Ephesians 6:12-18

As a Christian and from my own personal walk with God for many years, it can be very difficult to persuade any person in this day and age, to fight a supernatural fight. Secular thinking dismisses all talk of the supernatural realm as so much superstition hogwash, left over from the ancient world of idols and artefacts. At the same time, however, the advocates of all the occults have now stimulated people's curiosities, and have developed in many a fascination with evil rather than a determination to overcome it. For example the popular books of author J K Rowling, especially her series of 'Harry Potter' books, which sadly and unfortunately introduces our beautiful children all in the name of harmless fun and fantasy to an evil satanic world of Witchcraft, Sorcery, Satanism, the Occults, Wizards, Demons and the drinking of human blood to possess all this power that Harry Potter in the books and films portrays. The spiritual realm is not fantasy or fun it is a very dangerous place for any man, woman or child if they do not have protection. My help comes from the LORD. Where or who does your help come from—God or the devil? Who do you put your trust in times of trouble? Who is your hiding place; your refuge your rock, your anchor in the stormy seas of life? These are questions you can only answer for yourself. The Holy Bible tells us all, that it's better to put your whole trust in God rather than men!!!

Never-the-less, the Holy Bible is straightforward and declares that evil forces do exist in the spiritual realm that can have a substantial influence on the world and human events, like what you and I are seeing right now all over the world. Apostle Paul called them **'principalities'**.

Sometimes the presence of evil powers is evident, as in demon possession.

Luke 11:14 King James Version (KJV)

 [14] *"And he was casting out a devil, and it was dumb. And it came to pass, when the devil was gone out, the dumb spake; and the people wondered".*

However, Satan the Devil and his fallen angels have numerous ways to influence human activity and carry out their ultimate purpose, the capture of people and turn them away from God. Satan's tactics have never changed in his battle plans; he attacks the mind of a person because this is where the spiritual and physical battle takes place between good and evil. Satan knows if he can invade your thoughts with sinister evil satanic thoughts then he can control your mind to his way of thinking evil. By learning to refresh and renew our mind daily with the Holy Scriptures, with prayers, and *"standing firm"* by putting on the whole full armour of God Almighty. By wearing it and wielding our armaments of the double-edged sword (which is the very Word of God), and holding onto the mighty shield of faith and pleading the Blood of

Jesus Christ of Nazareth, we can resist the devil daily—for that evil serpent, the devil shall surely flee from us, AMEN!!!

We cannot be too careful about the idea we embrace in a satanic, un-godly, lustful society that embraces sex, power, fame and fortune much more than God's morality, love, grace, mercy and wisdom. Our best protection against the devil's deception and fiery darts onslaught is to have a firm, solid grounding in Biblical Truth. God's original desire and plan was for the first humans (Adam & Eve) to have dominion, rule and authority over all creation, and God's plan and desire has never changed for any human now on planet earth. But sin and rebellion made us incapable of carrying out that responsibility.

However, praise God, AMEN!

Jesus Christ of Nazareth, **'THE LORD OF LORDS', THE KING OF KINGS, 'THE GREAT I AM THAT I AM', 'THE HOLY ONE OF ISRAEL', 'THE MIGHTY MESSIAH', 'THE LAMB OF GOD', 'THE ROCK OF AGES', 'THE ANCIENT OF DAYS', 'THE LION OF THE TRIBE OF JUDAH', 'THE GOOD SHEPHERD', 'THE LIVING WORD', 'THE BREAD OF LIFE'** and 'THE WAY, THE TRUTH, AND THE LIFE', has opened the way for us all to re-establish our relationship with God and assume once again the responsibilities for which He created us.

- He has provided us with the forgiveness of our sins (JOHN 3:16-19).
- He has provided renewal for all of our life (2 CORINTHIANS 5:16-21).
- He has empowered us to carry out His work here on earth (ACTS 1:6-8).
- He has established helpful guidelines for proper conduct (1 JOHN2:7-17).

When we follow and obey God's commandments we experience true liberty, joy and peace. As His obedient children we can be fulfilled, fruitful and joyful as we look forward to the promise of eternal life, AMEN!

1 John 2:17 King James Version (KJV)

¹⁷ *"And the world passeth away, and the lust thereof: but he that doeth the will of God abideth for eve".*

Truthfulness, Clarity, Consistency, and Honesty are the **'Arrows of Faith'**, should be the basic qualities of Jesus Christ's followers. These are the things that last in the eyes of Almighty God, and they matter most evaluating Christian faith. We as Christians should offer nothing less! During times of trouble and calamity, it is sometimes difficult to remember or let alone stand upon the promises of God. The pressures of the moment may seem far overwhelming to you. At such times, remember it is often helpful to read and study and meditate upon, praying the entire chapter of the **Psalm of Life—Psalm 91.**

Psalm 91 King James Version (KJV)

¹ *"He that dwelleth in the secret place of the most High shall abide under the shadow of the Almighty.*

² *I will say of the LORD, He is my refuge and my fortress: my God; in him will I trust.*

³ *Surely he shall deliver thee from the snare of the fowler, and from the noisome pestilence.*

⁴ He shall cover thee with his feathers, and under his wings shalt thou trust: his truth shall be thy shield and buckler.

⁵ Thou shalt not be afraid for the terror by night; nor for the arrow that flieth by day;

⁶ Nor for the pestilence that walketh in darkness; nor for the destruction that wasteth at noonday.

⁷ A thousand shall fall at thy side, and ten thousand at thy right hand; but it shall not come nigh thee.

⁸ Only with thine eyes shalt thou behold and see the reward of the wicked.

⁹ Because thou hast made the LORD, which is my refuge, even the most High, thy habitation;

¹⁰ There shall no evil befall thee, neither shall any plague come nigh thy dwelling.

¹¹ For he shall give his angels charge over thee, to keep thee in all thy ways.

¹² They shall bear thee up in their hands, lest thou dash thy foot against a stone.

¹³ Thou shalt tread upon the lion and adder: the young lion and the dragon shalt thou trample under feet.

¹⁴ Because he hath set his love upon me, therefore will I deliver him: I will set him on high, because he hath known my name.

¹⁵ He shall call upon me, and I will answer him: I will be with him in trouble; I will deliver him, and honour him.

¹⁶ With long life will I satisfy him, and shew him my salvation".

Prayers for the Renewing of your Mind

Father God, I decree and I declare in Jesus Christ's anointed name that I have the mind of Christ, the Mighty Messiah, and I hold onto the thoughts, feelings and purposes of Christ's heart.

I thank You that I shall prosper and be in good health, even as my soul prospers. I trust in You LORD, with all of my heart, and mind, spirit and soul; I lean not unto my own understanding, but in all of my ways I acknowledge You, and You shall direct my paths. Today, I shall be transformed by the renewing of my mind that I may prove what is that good, and acceptable and perfect will of God. Your Word, LORD, shall not depart out of my mouth; but I shall meditate on it morning, noon and night that I might observe to do all that is written within the Word, for then I shall make my way prosperous, and I shall have good success in life. My thoughts are the thoughts of a diligent one, which tends only to plenteousness. Therefore, I am not anxious about anything, but in everything by prayers and petitions with thanksgiving, I present my requests to You Almighty God. And the peace of God, which transcends all understanding, will guard my heart and my mind in Jesus Christ's faithful name. Today, I fix my mind on by the Blood of Jesus Christ to whatever is true, whatever is worthy of reverence and is honourable and seemly, whatever is lovely and loveable, whatever is kind and winsome and gracious. If there is any virtue and excellence, if there is anything worthy of praise, I will think on and weigh and take account of these things. Today I roll all my works upon You, LORD—I commit and trust them wholly to You, and You will cause all my thoughts to become agreeable to Your perfect will, and so shall all my plans be established and successful, in Jesus Christ's loving and faithful name I pray, AMEN & AMEN & AMEN!!!

At all times, remember that faith comes by hearing, and hearing by the Word of God.

(ROMANS 10:17)

GOD'S WAY OF SALVATION FOR ALL MANKIND

 "Salvation is found in no-one else, for there is no other name under Heaven given to men by which we must be saved." *(Acts 4:12)*

 "Christ Jesus came into this world to save sinners." *(1Timothy 1:15)*

 "God wants all men/women to be saved and to come to the knowledge of truth". *(1Timothy 2:4)*

 "We testify that the Father has sent His Son to be the Saviour of the world." *(1 John 4:14)*

"What must I do to be saved? Believe in the Lord Jesus Christ, and *you* will be saved." *(Acts 16:30-31)*

"If we confess our sins, He is faithful and just to forgive us our sins and purify us from all unrighteousness." *(1 John 1:9)*

"If *you* confess with *your* mouth, "Jesus is Lord", and believe in *your* heart that God has raised Him from the dead, *you* will be saved. For it is with *your* heart *you* believe and are justified, and it is with *your* mouth that you confess and are saved. Everyone who calls on the name of the Lord will be saved." *(Romans 10:9-10, 13)*

"In reply Jesus declared, "I tell *you* the truth, no-one can see the Kingdom of God unless he is born Again . . . *You* must be born again." *(John 3 verses 3 and 7)*

THE BIBLE SAYS THERE IS ONLY ONE WAY TO HEAVEN

Jesus said, "I am the Way, the Truth, and the Life: no man/woman cometh unto the Father, but by me."(John 14:6)

Nobody except Jesus Christ Can Save Your Soul

- Admit *you're* a sinner in need of a Saviour.
- Be willing to turn from *your* sin **(repent)**.
- Believe that Jesus Christ died for *you* personally, was buried and rose from the dead on the third day.
- Through a simple sincere prayer, invite Jesus Christ into *your* life to become *your* Lord and personal Saviour.

WHAT TO PRAY

"Dear Lord Jesus, I come to You right now a sinner in need of a Saviour. I ask You to forgive me of all my sins, and wash me in Your precious blood. I accept Christ's sacrifice as perfect and complete. I ask Jesus Christ to come into my life, to change my life and to be my very best friend. I place my trust in Him alone for my salvation. Thank You for giving me eternal life, and thank You for writing my name in the Lamb's Book of Life. I believe now, I am Born Again, a brand new creation in Christ in God, and I ask You Lord Jesus, that Your Holy Spirit will fill me now with Your love, from the crown of my head to the soles of my feet, in Jesus Christ's magnificent name!"—**AMEN.**

Did *you* pray this prayer and accept Jesus Christ into *your* heart as *your very own* personal Saviour? If *your* answer was yes, then I personally congratulate *you* my friend, for this is just the beginning of a wonderful brand new life with Jesus Christ.

Now more importantly:

- *You* must read your Holy Bible everyday to get to know Jesus Christ better.
- Pray to God everyday (in *your* own words).
- Be water-baptised (full immersion under the baptismal waters) as soon as possible.
- Worship and fellowship, and serve with other Christians in a church where Christ is preached and the Holy Bible is the final authority.
- Finally, *you* must tell others about the love of Jesus Christ.

God bless you my brother/sister you are now a Born Again Christian in the Body of Christ—AMEN!!!

Sia Kuyembeh is a Christian author, song writer and singer. Her passion is to touch lives through her book ministry as she promotes the good news of the Gospel of Jesus Christ. She has a vision of taking Jesus Christ to all nations, and she is asking everyone by God's grace who is interested in this vision to join her in the mission field. This book is her first publication.

If you have been blessed by this book and you would like to contact the author, *Sia Kuyembeh* for more information concerning her books or ministry please send an email to this address below: